MW01180995

Step Up
Insights for Impactful
L e a d e r s h i p

Bayo Adewole

authorHOUSE™

1663 LIBERTY DRIVE, SUITE 200
BLOOMINGTON, INDIANA 47403
(800) 839-8640
WWW.AUTHORHOUSE.COM

© 2006 Bayo Adewole. All rights reserved.

No part of this book may be reproduced, stored in a retrieval system, or transmitted by any means without the written permission of the author.

First published by AuthorHouse 4/26/2006
ISBN: 1-4259-0592-7 (sc)

Library of Congress Control Number: 2005910848

Printed in the United States of America
Bloomington, Indiana

This book is printed on acid-free paper.

ACKNOWLEDGEMENT

God is most worthy of all my gratitude. For His Grace that brought me into His marvelous light and is building me up in knowledge and wisdom according to His purpose, my debt of gratitude cannot be repaid. God sent many of His children my way to bring this work to fruition.

I thank God for the love that He taught us all, which they have so generously showered on me. Pastor Yinka Adebiyi gave valuable suggestions to improve the material. Pastor Leke Sanusi was full of encouragement and kind words. Dr. Okey Onuzo read the manuscript more than once. Pastor Sola Fola-Alade, Tunde Irukera, Ayo Okesanya, Isoken Aiwerioba, Bayo Awe, Malcolm Fabiyi and Gbenga Oketona sacrificed time and energy to review the work. I am grateful for your labor of love. But as must be noted, I will be solely responsible for any shortcomings of this book.

Sincere appreciation to "Daddy G.O" - Pastor Enoch A. Adeboye, the General Overseer of the Redeemed Christian Church of God for accepting to review the manuscript and write the foreword. Your kindness and goodwill testifies to being a father indeed.

The Redeemed Christian Church of God, Jesus House Chicago members deserve much appreciation for the warm fellowship that we share together. I am grateful for the opportunity of being your pastor. Much of the material in this book came from teaching modules presented to the Workers of Zone 7 of the RCCG North America in June 2003 and I thank all the pastors and members of the zone for the opportunity to have been a part of that program.

I acknowledge the contributions and support of my immediate family in completing this work. My unique and precious gifts from God are Pastor Mrs. Funmi Adewole, Moyinoluwa, Ayooluwa and Inioluwa. Thank you for all your love.

FOREWORD

Leadership is one of the most dangerous things a person can aspire to. Yet almost every human being wants to lead. Leadership demands humility, accountability and a high sense of responsibility and integrity. People have tried to learn the skills of leadership and we have heard about the leadership styles of many leaders.

Ultimately however, it is the spiritual principles that can make or mar a leader. Pastor Bayo Adewole in this book has carefully set forth these principles using Nehemiah as the main stay of his exposition on leaders and aspirants. You will benefit from reading this book.

The story of Nehemiah is indeed a very good anchor on which to hang a work of this nature, for all the principles are aptly illustrated by his thought processes and actions. Read Nehemiah, then read this book – STEP UP: INSIGHTS FOR IMPACTFUL LEADERSHIP.

You will then see why every leader must lead with the utmost care and attention; the Bible says "with fear and trembling". You will be blessed by reading this book.

Pastor E.A. Adeboye
General Overseer : Redeemed Christian Church of God Worldwide
February 2005

"Flowers are beautiful, but their ultimate purpose is to produce fruits. At the right time flowers must give way to fruits"

Rev. George Adegboye

CONTENTS

I. INTRODUCTION   **1**
What is Leadership?   2

II. WHY STEP UP?   **3**
God Commands Change   3
God is Doing a New Thing   3
We Have Capacity for Greater Things   4
There's a World to Win   5
There are Mysteries to Search Out   5
The Next Level is Beyond the Present   6

III. HOW NEHEMIAH DID IT   **8**
Nehemiah had a Burden   8
Nehemiah Prepared Himself   9
Nehemiah Prepared the People   10
Nehemiah was Determined   12

IV. NEHEMIAH'S DISTINGUISHING CHARACTERS   **13**
Love of the People   13
Wisdom and Humility   14
Integrity   14
Discretion   14
Love of God   15
A Man of Prayer   16
A Happy Man   16

V. TEN LIFE LESSONS FROM NEHEMIAH   **17**
Recognize the Problem You are Called to Solve   17
Focus on the Source of all Power   18
Be Bold   20
Keep the Vision   22
There Will be Sacrifices to Make   24
Prepare for Risks   26
Win the Confidence of the People   27

It's About Service   29
Your Integrity is Critical   30
God is Your Provider   31

VI. DEALING WITH ADVERSARIES   **33**
So, What Does the Adversary Want?   38

VII. A WORD FOR FOLLOWERS   **40**

VIII. NUGGETS ON LEADERSHIP   **43**
BELIEVE IT, YOU ARE A LEADER!   43
LEARN THE VISION OF YOUR TEAM/GROUP   44
IDENTIFY WITH THE PEOPLE   45
DELEGATE RESPONSIBILITY AS NECESSARY   45
BE REAL   46
MAINTAIN A BALANCE IN YOUR LIFE   47
BE DECISIVE   48
PROVE YOURSELF AS A LEADER IN THE FAMILY   49

IX. CONCLUSION   **50**

STEP UP - INSIGHTS FOR IMPACTFUL LEADERSHIP
I. INTRODUCTION

Great potentials lie in everyone. We are all offered opportunities or avenues to make the potentials in each of us become realities. Opportunities are circumstances or situations that offer an advantage or benefit. A person who consistently recognizes such opportunities and uses them, excels in whatsoever he does. But we must understand that life is a long race lived in stages. Children are born nearly helpless with seemingly no ability to care for themselves, let alone change things around them, but it does not take long for the potentials in the children to manifest. When hungry or uncomfortable, a child cries and then begins to make motions that draw attention to the need. A child progresses to the next level by moving and by reaching for things where they are close enough. There is a progression to successive levels by a child and many times the parents would not be able to say when a change took place, but would note the distinct change that had taken place.

Over time, the changes or transition to subsequent levels, become slower. Because the parents expect them, they are no longer as obvious when they occur. By the time one is grown, the changes are not as dramatic and many may not be making the necessary changes and progression that are critical to complete development. In spiritual growth, we experience development very much like new born babies. Our Father watches us closely for those vital signs of progression that lead us to attaining His goals for creating and saving us. No wonder God Himself had to tell His people the Israelites in Deuteronomy 2:3 *"you have been wandering around in this hill country long enough"*.

It was time to move to the next level.

Movement is a vital sign of life and extended motionlessness inevitably results in death. Change is a form of movement and when we fail to move we stagnate. Even when some animals hibernate, they get active as soon as the

1

season of hibernation is over. The Dead Sea is so called because it receives all that comes in, but flows nowhere – all that comes into it comes to rest in it. Yet it is common that people remain where they are, apparently motionless. No matter what achievements one has attained, life continues to offer us new opportunities that God expects us to use for His glory.

There are many reasons why people may not be moving on to the next level of life. An obvious one is a lack of vision. Not knowing that there is a higher or better level to attain makes some people remain where they are. Fear or lack of confidence is another reason some people hold on to what they have, and so are not willing to reach for the greater things available to them. A third reason may have to do with motivation. Not being motivated enough could leave one complacent in the same position even though the continuing change around demands a re-adjustment of one's priorities at the minimum. Finally, people will not move to the next level without good leaders.

We are living in an age and generation that is devoid of good and effective leadership. Good leadership is needed in families, churches, businesses, governments and anywhere that people are working towards an objective. Sadly, there are few good examples of strong leadership in society. Good leadership harnesses and inspires the people to work with one another and bring out their individual gifts to jointly achieve that needed move to the next level in different areas of their lives.

What is Leadership?

Defined simply, leadership is influence; it is the ability to bring people together and inspire them to do what they ought to do. Good Leaders can, without force or coercion encourage people to follow, even when they do not want to. God Himself is the ultimate leader who has called every believer to teach others and thereby lead them to Him. Leaders are not born, they are created by the same circumstances that everyone goes through. The right to lead is not necessarily by election or appointment; it is usually earned over a period of time.

This book is a study in the leadership skills of a man in the Bible named Nehemiah. It is a study of the book in the Bible by the same name. Nehemiah took the nation of Israel to a new level after the devastation of war. Figuratively speaking, the book mirrors our lives, careers, families, ministries and the church. It re-emphasizes the key role that leadership plays in the lives of people, within the church and in the world at large.

II. WHY STEP UP?

We have heard it repeatedly said that change is the only thing that is guaranteed in life. But knowing about something and living it out can be remarkably different. Accepting change is difficult for most people. Leaders may be somewhat better in this regard since they are instruments of change. But leaders also need to appreciate the ramifications of change. Variety is good and many enjoy it when it relates to our food and clothing. Sometimes, we do not appreciate variety in our work, lifestyle, attitudes and relationships.

God Commands Change

God commands change. God's expectation of His children is that they desire Him more and more. God wants His children to walk closely with Him; He told Abraham

"I am the Almighty God, walk before me and be thou perfect"[1].

God wants His children to go higher and be more like Him. To the children of Israel He said, *"you have been wandering around this hill country long enough; turn northward"[2].*

Without change, life and our service would be like a circling motion, in which no ground is covered and there is no fulfillment. Our Christian life is like a race. When we give our lives to Christ, we begin the race and until the appearing of our Lord Jesus, the race is not complete. The end of our race will be in heaven, God reveals in the book of Revelation 2:10 that we will receive the reward for all that we do on earth. The reward for winning a soul will be different from the reward for winning ten souls for the Kingdom. So we must work while it is day. God gives the vision for every season and people. We must position ourselves to be instruments for achieving God's purpose and ultimately receiving the desired reward for our service.

God is Doing a New Thing

"See, I am doing a new thing! Now it springs up; do you not perceive it? I am making a way in the desert and streams in the wasteland."

This truth found in Isaiah 43:19 is so profound. Its import is that if you do not get involved with the new thing that God is doing, He will leave you out of it. It also means that living in the old is like running our agenda or plan. God may not have been in it, and if He was, He might have since moved on to another thing. God is not the author of confusion, He promised that He will not do a thing without revealing it to His prophets (Amos 3:7). However, when He has revealed it and we hold on to the old, He will find the people who will receive the new vision and walk in it.

"Because of the Lord's great love we are not consumed, for His compassions never fail. They are new every morning; great is your faithfulness"[3]

God provides fresh anointing for each day; the blessings of yesterday are not planned for today. This is because God who knows all things has determined that yesterday's blessings will not do for today.

We Have Capacity for Greater Things
No matter how good our past has been, our future can be greater and this is the plan of God for us. When we settle into the good and have no desire for the best, God is not glorified.

"The path of the righteous is like the first gleam of dawn, shining ever brighter till the full light of day"[4].

Being content is a good virtue, in fact the Bible describes it as great gain – 1 Timothy 6:6, but not appropriating the blessings of God is wasteful. We can be content and at the same time reach out for the gifts of God meant for us. This comes with an attitude of service, when the motivation for pressing on is not self-glorification. Better should be the end of a thing than the beginning, according to Ecclesiastes 7:8. Our Lord Jesus taught that it is only those who complete the race that will receive the reward (Matthew 13). Life is a marathon, it requires perseverance; sustaining power that ensures that we complete the race with even greater zeal than we started with.

Christians are to bear fruits. Our fruitfulness, must progress to more fruit and from more fruit to much fruit. Jesus said that we are the planting of the Lord, any tree that does not bear fruit, the Father, who is the husbandman will cut off. Any tree that bears fruits, he will prune that it might bear more fruit. Hallelujah! A tree that bears fruits one year and then stops bearing fruits in subsequent years will most probably have to go. Bearing fruits is the evidence of remaining in the will of God for our lives. As Jesus said,

"I am the vine, you are the branches. If a man remains in me and I in him, he will bear much fruit; apart from me, you can do nothing"[5].

If we abide in Him then the fruit must come. And He has said that He will prune the tree so it can bear more fruit and more fruit must improve and produce much fruit. The One who made us wants continuous productivity from our lives. He desires it, He prepares us for it and will help us to bring it forth. We are designed not to remain as we started, but to move from one level to a higher level and again to another higher level. Stagnation is the prelude to regression.

God intends to remove the dross that the vessel might come forth finer for Him - Proverbs 25:4. Many still have dross that needs to be removed, the scum of the old man (doubt, selfishness, anger and pride) need to be taken away so that the vessel that God can use will emerge.

There's a World to Win
The world is not yet fully won for Jesus. There are still parts of the world where the gospel cannot be preached freely. The light of the gospel has not quite broken through the barriers of false religions which hold billions, may be up to half of the world in bondage of sin and ignorance. Even in the free world, the weak testimony of the Church is leading to a resurgence of disguised pagan worship, new age religion and unspeakable immorality. God makes it clear that He does not want the destruction of the wicked. It is His will that all will come to the knowledge of the saving grace of Jesus Christ. But how will they hear if there is no one to take the gospel to them. God needs an army. His army needs leaders. An army that has not got the vision of what God wants to do is not useful in His hands. We must come out of the lethargic state and rise up to the yearnings of God's heart. The end will not come because you and I have heard and received the gospel. The end will come only when the whole earth has heard the gospel. We must see ourselves as the instruments that God will use to reach the whole earth. When we pray for the salvation of souls around the world, we should also pray that we will be willing vessels in His hand to reach all nations and peoples for His Kingdom.

There are Mysteries to Search Out
There are yet deep mysteries that God wants to reveal to His people. But He reveals Himself only to those who seek Him.

"It is the glory of God to conceal a matter; to search out a matter is the glory of kings"[6].

We will be failing in our responsibility as kings if we do not search out in the secret place, the deep things that God has hidden. He who taught us not to cast our pearls before swine will not cast His precious word/vision to any one He knows will not be obedient.

To be relevant, we must go up higher in the things of God. We live in an age of knowledge and progress. The gospel must be relevant to new challenges and issues that face the people today. We cannot offer the solutions of the past for new challenges, just like we cannot pour new wine into old wineskin or it will break. We know that the word of God is complete, it is able to address issues that confront people today, but we need our teacher, the Holy Spirit to expound and make plain the mind of God concerning them. When the Church does not speak as one about any matter, the rest of the people find good reason not to listen. The Spirit of God is one and God is in control. Using human wisdom will lead to ridicule, God wants His people to come up higher and closer to Him.

It is a challenge we must accept. The children of Israel rejected God's appeal to come up higher when they said they would rather have God communicate with them through Moses. They did not want to come before the Lord on the mountain. At the end of the day, they only got to know God's acts while Moses got to know God's ways. They ended up perishing in the wilderness. We really have one choice for successful Christian living; to go on to the next level in God.

The Next Level is Beyond the Present
"No eye has seen, no ear has heard, no mind has conceived what God has prepared for those who love Him"[7].

God is able to do exceedingly, abundantly beyond that which we can think or imagine, through His power that is at work in us. God's plans are far greater than we can know. They can only be received by faith. Being people who appreciate physical things more than spiritual reality, we are often captivated by the good that God has provided for us. The Lord gives us the much that we can manage at a time, so we do not destroy ourselves. Almost without exception, we tend to become content with the good things, when God is preparing the best for us. At other times, it is just the fear of failure or the intimidating posture of present circumstances that makes us accept where we are and conclude that things cannot change.

"Do not be afraid, little flock, for your Father has been pleased to give you the kingdom"[8].
We are to live in dominion, exercising authority over situations and circumstances, not lacking anything good and being fulfilled in all that we do.

The next level is attained by taking a leap of faith to begin something nobody, including ourselves, thought was possible. Whatever it is that we are involved in, until we reach the pinnacle of it, God has not finished His work yet. In the eyes of men, we may have excelled and attained all that is possible, but we must keep in mind that God wants to do what is beyond the minds of people. He can and will do what will make the ears of those that hear to tingle.

"No one from the east or the west or from the desert can exalt a man. But it is God who judges: He brings one down, He exalts another"[9]

Effectiveness and productivity could be one person's next level, while for another it may be getting started with the vision that God has for him. God is interested in increase. Even where we have received the vision and are already running with it, God desires to display His best through us. We can become smarter, sharper and reach further. Moving to the next level in our individual lives would lead to more of the fruit of the Spirit. In the family, it will lead to unity and love, making our homes places of His dwelling. The next level moves us closer to God, that we may profit from the revelation of His word and obedience to Him.

Our ministries need to move to the next level in reaching new groups and even nations and bringing people from every nation into the Kingdom. We will consolidate our successes and reinforce God's army, making it equipped and effective for today's battle.

III. HOW NEHEMIAH DID IT

Leadership is like most things in life. No one is born with it. Exposure, experience and a desire to become a leader would make one person better than another in leading other people. We want to choose to walk the road Nehemiah walked, to learn from his experience. God fulfills His role by arranging situations that will sharpen us. However, the first step in wanting to lead is often the most difficult and is pivotal to making leaders out of ordinary people.

In Biblical times and even today, the feeling of inadequacy is the greatest mountain before potential leaders. There seems to be a myth that leaders are cast from a different mold. The ordinary person feels that he just does not have what it takes. This feeling of inadequacy is a good starting point indeed, because if we think we have what it takes then we probably will not learn what needs to be learned. So the ordinary person has the potential of becoming a leader because everything can be learned. Ordinarily, this should make everyone comfortable about leadership, but we know that not everyone can or wants to lead. The more amenable you are to the requirements of leadership, the further you will go as a leader and the larger will be your capacity to lead.

A family is a group of individuals that need to channel their efforts and resources to achieve set goals, but many family heads do not see the need to learn leadership principles for their responsibilities in the home. This poor perception of the need, makes many to simply lead by what they see other people (parents, relations and neighbors) do. The better the perception of the need to learn (usually from the feeling of inadequacy), the more we give ourselves to learning and making needed changes. Consequently, we become more effective as leaders.

Let us go on the road that Nehemiah went and find out truths that will help us lead other people more effectively.

Nehemiah had a Burden

Those who fail to prepare have prepared to fail. Success comes to those who make plans and work their plans. It is hardly ever a chance occurrence. The situation at hand was the reproach upon God's people, the children of Israel, and Jerusalem the city of God. The enemies of Israel had attacked Jerusalem and destroyed her walls. The people were now afflicted – they were in poverty and shame and scattered abroad. God's people were defenseless, their situation was unattractive, there was no organized society and they were in a seemingly hopeless situation.

Nehemiah was himself a slave in a foreign land. He learned of the situation of his people from asking those who recently fled Jerusalem. His first reaction to the news was deep sorrow. He quickly went into a period of fasting and praying, making intercession to God about the situation. Nehemiah gave priority to what was most important: speaking to God and getting to know the mind of God about the situation. Because the need was already in the mind of God, there was an accelerated answer to his prayer.

Nehemiah appeared before his master the king as usual, but King Artaxerxes recognized that Nehemiah was sorrowful. It seemed like God's timing was ahead of Nehemiah's timing because God immediately answered his prayer when the king asked what help he, Nehemiah, would require to fulfill the purpose of God.

Nehemiah seized the opportunity offered by the king. His request was quite articulate – time off from his duties, support from the governors of regions through which he would travel back to Jerusalem and provision of materials for the work. Clearly, Nehemiah had been thinking about what would be needed for the task. He must have seen himself being actively involved in bringing deliverance to his people. God answered his prayer and the King favored him and honored every one of his requests.

Nehemiah Prepared Himself
Now, even though the favor of God was upon Nehemiah, he did not rush into the vision. He made sure he understood its full ramifications. Nehemiah spent more time in God's presence, and for some time he did not tell any man what was on his mind.

"I had not told anyone what my God had put in my heart to do for Jerusalem".

Then he went on to Jerusalem and to the ruins of the wall. He assessed the damage by night. He noted the state of the gates, he identified peculiar details of the situation, like areas that animals (transportation) could not go through. He was there three days, going over the work at hand and understanding the requirements better. He did not confer with anybody so that they would not discourage or affect his resolve to do the work.

The preparation of Nehemiah is in tune with what Jesus taught in Luke 14, that no man goes to battle without first assessing the capabilities of his enemy, and no man starts to build a tower without first finding out the cost, lest he begins and is unable to complete it.

Preparation is critical and if you do not have a plan from the beginning, you get caught up in details that lead nowhere. Get a plan and work the plan.

Paul also taught about the principle of not conferring with 'flesh and blood' until the vision has become clear. After God had spoken to him, he went into the desert alone. That time of being alone with God provides you the opportunity of getting the picture like no-one else can give it. The picture that God will give you, will keep you focused as a leader. It will help you develop God's eye for the goal and provides the assurance that you will get there.

The favor of God and the King must have made Nehemiah very enthusiastic. He could have just moved on, knowing that God had already signed on. He however recognized the nature of God, and that God leads His people "precept by precept". He continued to wait on God in prayer to receive specific instructions that he would need along the way. When God uses a man, He is the one at work. The person does not have all the answers to all the issues that will come up - God does. The time of intimate communion with God about the purpose, sharpens the vision for the leader, but the complete details are known to God only.

"It is not by strength that one prevails"[2].

Nehemiah Prepared the People

A vision as big as that given to Nehemiah could not have been accomplished by any one individual. Leadership is about influencing other people to achieve a given purpose. Many times, the leader would understand the purpose better than the people, but without the people the leader would not be able to accomplish the goal. Nehemiah started very much like Jesus did, by taking a small group and grounding them in the purpose at hand[3]. John Maxwell says that "One is too small a number to achieve anything".

Next, Nehemiah expounded the vision that God had put in his heart to the people. He urged them to come together and work to remove their reproach. He encouraged them with the testimonies of God's favor and the blessing from King Artaxerxes for the work. By the working of the Spirit of God, the people received the vision with gladness and committed themselves to working with Nehemiah. He urged them to also prepare, both physically and spiritually. The advantage seen in their preparation is the unity of the leadership and the led. Unity unleashes a special anointing for outstanding achievements[4].

Clearly the people received understanding and put away any differences and chose to walk in love with one another.

"They replied, 'Let us start building.' So they began this good work"[5].

Different groups of people got involved in the work. In the third chapter of the book of Nehemiah, we see that the categories of people involved in the work were sons and daughters (young people), Levites (priests), gate-keepers, goldsmiths and merchants. There was room for all the groups as long as they were of the same mind, willing to be used to remove the reproach on Jerusalem and God's people. The only people left out of the work were the adversaries and haughty nobles. Nehemiah said to his adversaries – Sanballat and Tobiah,

"But, as for you, you have no share in Jerusalem or any claim or historic right to it"[6].

As long as the heart was right, the hands were useful and welcome.

Nehemiah had to organize the different groups to do the work. He did it in a simple manner that was also convenient for the people. He allocated sections of the work to families. Each family had a portion of the work assigned to them based on their number and what they could complete. Notice in chapter 3 that not everyone in each family was involved. There were some "nobles" who were too proud to get involved, and so they were simply ignored[7]. There was no bitterness or animosity against them. The work was not only rebuilding the broken walls; but also the reconstruction of the gates, the towers of furnaces, doors and locks also had to be repaired or replaced. The work was allocated with these details in mind. The organization of the work, called for order and accountability as well as a system of reporting and monitoring.

Nehemiah himself got involved at the grassroots[8]. He did not consider himself too big for manual work. He got involved just like the other people. Leadership by example is very effective in influencing people. The life that a leader lives speaks much louder than the words that he or she speaks. If you do not speak and just show what you want done, people will follow. Whatever the leader is, the people will eventually reflect. Leadership is not about instructing others, it is about influencing them, and the most effective way to influence people is to just live the life or be the example to follow.

Nehemiah was Determined

Nehemiah was determined to reach his God given destiny. Opposition to the vision he had received arose quickly and sharply. Nehemiah tried to walk in understanding without allowing their actions to affect him or the work. He was discerning about the actions of the opposition and made appropriate responses. He responded verbally; then he set a watch and finally, he armed his men[9]. The most significant aspect of his actions though was to put the matter before God in prayer[10].

Nehemiah was a man of prayer, He was guided by the word of God. Nehemiah's desire was to please God. He had an understanding of living a life of service and he lived a righteous life with outstanding zeal to do the will of God.

IV. NEHEMIAH'S DISTINGUISHING CHARACTERS

The personal qualities of a leader are important because when they are magnified in the process of leading others, they become the qualities of the group and could make for greatness or mediocrity. Before becoming a leader, personal issues must first be brought under control, otherwise the leader is literally being set-up for failure. Personal issues here refer to matters of family relationships, discipline and honor. In summary a leader must be a person of integrity. Maturity in dealing with one's personal affairs should precede being saddled with a higher responsibility that involves showing the way to others. Additional responsibilities should be progressively increased as abilities, skills and confidence is developed. Good personal qualities form the bedrock of good leadership. Nehemiah had personal traits that enhanced his leadership and aided him to carry out his responsibilities while at the same time endearing him to the people.

Love of the People

Nehemiah was a loving man. His love for the people was very deep. The primary purpose of his mission to Jerusalem (rebuilding the wall) was not for his benefit directly, because he did not live in Jerusalem. He stepped up to the challenge facing the people in an attitude of service. He was not seeking to be served. Nehemiah 5:16 says that he drew no official food allowance for twelve years during which he served as governor in Jerusalem. This was directly opposed to the attitude of previous leaders who took advantage of the people to enrich themselves. When the people were suffering under the burden of interest charges by the rich, he found a way to relieve their suffering. He provoked love among the people and those who had been charging their brethren interest on loans, agreed to forgo it[1].

Love for his people was so intense that he fed about 150 people regularly from his resources. He willingly gave himself and his resources for the good of the people. While leading them, he worked alongside the people. Nehemiah 5: 16 says

"I devoted myself to work on this wall".

He was not an armchair leader; he was out on the field working side by side with the people. Whatever was required, if he had it, he gave it. And what he didn't have, he sought from those who did.

Wisdom and Humility

Wisdom and humility can be gleaned from the actions of Nehemiah. During the course of the rebuilding of the wall, he organized the work for effectiveness. He changed strategies when it was necessary. He ensured that his people were carried along and stayed focused on the work. After the wall was completed and dedicated to God, Nehemiah would have stayed on as governor, but it was never his goal to become a ruler. He was humble enough to stick to the original plan which was to serve the needs at hand. He left Jerusalem to go back to his responsibility as a cup-bearer for King Artaxerxes of Babylon. In wisdom, he arranged for how to re-populate Jerusalem. He set a target for 10% of the people of every tribe to return to Jerusalem so the city could be inhabited and repopulated.

Integrity

Integrity was a key personal quality of Nehemiah. He kept his promise to his boss whom God had used to show him remarkable favor when he was starting the project. He returned to the King, despite the obvious attraction of becoming a governor in his own right. The integrity of Nehemiah made him respected throughout the land. He was in a position to correct even the priests where they went wrong [2]. He felt responsible for the people that he led. At every instance, he did what he could to defend their interest. The people he appointed to work with him were people of integrity - Hanani his brother who filled-in as governor while he returned to Babylon was a man who feared God [3]. When Nehemiah needed to sanction anyone, he did so with integrity. His reputation as a just and fair man made it possible for him to act freely and decisively.

Nehemiah was accountable though he had no direct boss as far as the reconstruction of the wall of Jerusalem was concerned. He maintained records of all that he did. He recognized that the resources that were placed at his disposal were to be kept in trust for the people. He made sure that God's favor and blessings for the people, which was entrusted in him, was not abused. Records of people, materials and actions taken in the course of the work, were kept for posterity. Being accountable is a safeguard for the leader, for it helps prevent abuse of office and provides a defense against accusations.

Discretion

Discretion gives the leader opportunity to relate with God and settle issues ahead of time. A discreet leader is not quick to bring to the general group issues he is yet to clear with the Lord. Nehemiah spent time understanding what God had called him to do. He kept it to himself till the direction for action was clear. The danger in not praying before sharing is that you may not know where your leading is coming from once you have made the matter public. Once the matter is public, the leader is subject to different influences, which may make it difficult to understand and follow God's leading. Being discreet does not preclude discussing with others, but it requires few words most of which must be with the Lord. Nehemiah's words to the adversary and his people were few. He spent more time in prayer.

Love of God

Nehemiah was a man who loved God. This was his passion. Nehemiah lived at a time when the people had been scattered and there was a strong influence of the cultures of their neighbors on them. He kept the instructions of God and whenever he saw his brethren living in sin, it grieved him. He got the people to recommit themselves to the laws of God. He was not a priest, but he made many reforms that turned the hearts of the people back to God.

Some of these were:

- to obey the laws of Moses [4];
- not to marry or give in marriage to pagan neighbors [5];
- to keep and maintain the sanctity of the Sabbath day [6];
- to pay the annual Temple tax [7];
- not to do any work in the seventh year and to cancel the debts owed by other Jews [8];
- to bring the first part of every harvest to the Lord's temple [9];
- to give their eldest sons and the first born of all herds and flocks to God [10];
- to bring a tithe of the best of their flour and other grain offerings, the best of their wines and olive oils.

They were encouraged to bring a tithe of everything the land produced to the Lord [11].

These changes were willingly endorsed by the people. It must have been that his own love for God inspired them to love God too. He had knowledge of the goodness of God to his people and so he made sure that they focused on God.

Soon after the completion of the wall of Jerusalem, he organized the people to listen to the reading of the word of God. This was from a desire to bring them up to a higher level of spiritual understanding. He wanted them to return to their heavenly security by putting God in His place in their lives, so that it would be well with them.

A Man of Prayer

Nehemiah was a man of prayer. He commenced the leadership of his people by praying to God [12]. He understood the principles of prayer. He was quick to repent for he recognized that their afflictions were as a result of sin. He knew what God's promises were concerning His people. He believed that God would honor His word and so he regularly sought the face of God concerning issues that he came across. He prayed at his desperate moments, when he wanted to start and when the enemy appeared to be formidable against him. Nehemiah also learnt to pray during his relatively peaceful times. He constantly asked God's favor for himself. He reminded God of His deeds at his intimate times of worship. He did not fail to add to his memorial before God [13]. Without a doubt, God answered his prayers. God showed him the intentions of his adversaries so he could pre-empt them. God stirred the people to work with him and God fulfilled his mission for him. A personal prayer life is very critical to succeeding in leadership.

A Happy Man

Finally, Nehemiah was a happy man, filled with the joy of the Lord and radiating it to people around him. The news of the ruins of Jerusalem changed his countenance and his boss said, he had never seen him sad or unhappy. Perhaps his cheerful disposition was such that his sadness about Jerusalem was noted by the striking contrast. The King wanted to do something about whatever was causing his servant to be sad and he wanted him back once it was settled. Everyone around him seemed to desire his company. It had to be the presence of God and God's favor that made him stand out from other people. Evidently, God was with Nehemiah because of his godly lifestyle. God's beauty was upon him and his joy was a testimony to those around him.

V. TEN LIFE LESSONS FROM NEHEMIAH

Lesson 1:
RECOGNIZE THE PROBLEM
YOU ARE CALLED TO SOLVE

Often we become so accustomed to our situation that we do not expect anything different. At other times, just being comfortable makes us ignore changes that are taking place all around us. Because people change too, it is difficult to know what meets one's expectation at any point in time. When one has been in a situation for a while, it is easy to conclude that things will not change. To make a difference in a situation, someone must first recognize what is wrong with the situation. To help us recognize problems, we need.

- To know our environment
- Be sensitive to changes around us
- Maintain a standard that does not change

These requirements are in fact God's perspective to His world. Consider these scriptures:

"Known unto God are all His works from the beginning of the world"[1]. *"Indeed, He who watches over Israel neither slumbers nor sleeps"[2]. "For the eyes of the Lord range throughout the earth to strengthen those whose hearts are fully committed to Him" [3]. "Jesus Christ is the same yesterday and today and forever"[4].*

God is the source of all knowledge, He is the creator of the universe. He is the one that grants grace, wisdom and ability to make a difference in the lives of other people. A close fellowship with Him will give us His perspective. He will show us where and how the lives of His people are falling short of His plan and their potentials.

Apostle Paul urges us

"Do not conform any longer to the pattern of this world, but be transformed by the renewing of your mind. Then you will be able to test and approve what God's will is - His good, pleasing and perfect will"[5].

He gave us the panacea for living a purposeful life that is pleasing unto God and beneficial to the world. Not being conformed to the world sharpens our sensitivity to discern what does not meet up with God's expectation. It keeps our standard intact - unchanged. The greatest motivation any leader can have is that the goal or purpose to which he is committed, is the will of God for his life.

Sin brought along many problems to the world. No single person is supposed to solve all the problems. Our Lord Jesus came to end the rule of Satan, but even that is for those who will believe on Him. Leaders are designed to solve particular problems of the people they are called to lead. As a leader, you must recognize which problem(s) God wants you to focus on. God knows it, so you should ask Him. God is the one that arranged for you to solve them. He has all you need to make the difference, so receive the strength and leading you need from Him.

When the heart of Nehemiah was stirred to make a difference, he went straight to God in prayer. He fasted to prepare himself. From the fourth verse of the first chapter of the book, Nehemiah poured out his heart before God. Clearly, he had an ongoing relationship with God. His passion for the people of God and for a restoration of their relationship with God was evident. Knowing God's expectations helped him to pray according to the will of God and he received answers to his prayer even quicker than he expected.

Lesson 2:
FOCUS ON THE SOURCE OF ALL POWER

Change is such a dominant phenomenon on earth, but ironically, most people resist change. It takes a lot of effort and will to bring about change. Even individuals who need change in their situation, often get frustrated when they consider the effort that is needed to bring about the desired change. By doing nothing, many people end up with what they do not want. When a leader comes along, they are willing to transfer the responsibility for the change to him, after all, there is now someone else to be held accountable if the desired change does not happen. This pre-supposes that the leader is super-human or how else can he come to take-on the responsibilities that many individuals find hard to tackle by themselves? The leader needs to tap into the source of all power, the Almighty God, to get the job done.

It is with God that nothing is impossible. Recognizing the source of power and drawing from that source is critical to success as a leader.

"Not by might nor by power, but by my Spirit,' says the LORD Almighty"[6] *"It is not by strength that one prevails"*[7].

These words make it clear that:
- There is a limit to the abilities of men
- The Spirit of God working through man can make a man accomplish all things

Leadership as was defined earlier is all about influencing people to achieve a goal. We know that God created man with a will, and in His image. The will that God gave to man is such a powerful gift that man often uses it against God his creator. That is what sin is. Willful disobedience to God or constituted authority in the world and the Church of God, happens everyday. Our world today speaks more of equality, freedom, independence and self-expression all of which encourage people to live their lives in ways that give them maximum pleasure. People do not want to follow any leader, yet without leaders, the people are like sheep without a shepherd and are easy prey to predators. God's word declares:

"The king's heart is in the hand of the Lord; He directs it like a water-course wherever He pleases"[8]

Can a leader work with people who are motivated by selfish objectives? Yes, if he has the help of God to touch their hearts about the goal. Once GOD steps in, the end is certain – it will be victory. Therefore, the real issue is what will make God step in? What does the leader have to do?

Even though God seeks a heart that is right before Him, to use to bring about deliverance or change to His people, He still expects the person to fully identify with the people. There can be no self righteousness before God. Nehemiah identified with the people and confessed their sins. The result of identifying with the people is that the leader receives the burden for the situation. It also brings passion as the leader receives and understands God's perspective of the matter. The leader gets intimate with God and so receives a deeper understanding of the power and faithfulness of God.

Moses got to know the ways of God, but the children of Israel only knew His acts. This made a fundamental difference in how Moses and the rest of the people reacted to the challenges that they faced. When the people would grumble and start talking about returning to Egypt, Moses was always confident that God had the solution for them, he would always run to God.

God is sovereign, therefore His purpose stands above every other. But, God's purposes are fitted into His timing. He created time and His plans are all within set time frames. Good plans will not make God step in. When a leader is motivated to do a new thing or move on to the next level, he must remember that to succeed, the Sovereign God has to take it over, for all things are for His pleasure. The projects and plans belong to Him and He gives instructions about what needs to be done. Simply put, you have to let go of your idea and plans for achieving the goal.

Remember that Moses, when he sought to deliver a fellow Jew who was being oppressed, ended up being a murderer who had to flee into the wilderness (Exodus 2).

Recognizing that God is the owner of the plan, the leader must take a very convenient position as a messenger or helper in the implementing process. He simply executes according to the instructions received. If the unexpected comes his way, he pauses to ask the owner what to do. The burden would thus be much reduced and there would be no fear of failure.

When a house is being built, the builders work off the plan of the house. A good builder will not even relocate a light switch without checking with the architect, not to talk of re-arranging the spaces in the house. The same approach has to be adopted for successful leadership. We need to get back as often as needed to be sure we are still building according to God's plan. In our case, God often does not hand over a beginning to end plan, because He knows us. The full plan remains in God's hands. We have to keep going back in prayer to get specifications for the next stage and clarification where it is needed. Do not go in your strength! The arm of flesh will fail (Isaiah 31:2-4).

Nehemiah returned to God regularly, and he did so mainly by studying the scripture. He ensured that he and his other leaders, knew the laws of Moses and he got them to commit to obeying them. That way, he kept them in line with the plan of God. He may not have had a working relationship with the Holy Spirit because of the age in which he lived. But now we have the Holy Spirit in us, and so we are better able to work with God on a daily basis, which should be to our advantage.

Today's leader has the unique benefit of having the Holy Spirit as a senior partner to teach, guide and lead him. God comes alongside the leader as with all His children, to lighten the burden of leadership for the willing leader. Indeed, the leader that men see is no more than a physical instrument, the Almighty God Himself is the One at work and He cannot fail.

Lesson 3:
BE BOLD
Great leaders confront major issues that intimidate other people. Without boldness, the simplest of changes will seem unachievable. The comfort zone is a place where we all long to be. We know what comes next, how it is going to come, what we will do about it and what the results will be. But wait, the Bible says that

"But hope that is seen is no hope at all. Who hopes for what he already has?"[9]

Nothing of significance will be achieved in the comfort zone. We are required to step out in faith, trusting God to work through us.

"For God did not give us a spirit of timidity, but a spirit of power, of love and of self-discipline"[10]. "The righteous are as bold as a lion"[11].

Our Father and King is the Lion of the tribe of Judah. Fear is of the devil and it is what the devil uses to rule the world. That is why we meet more people who say it cannot be done; no-one has done it before, they are too powerful for us, or to use the Bible story of the spies that Moses sent

"We seemed like grasshoppers in our own eyes, and we looked the same to them"[12].

Boldness does not mean reckless behavior, rather it speaks of sound judgment based on knowledge of the word of God and experience of His faithfulness. We wonder how it was that the three Hebrew youngsters could say to the king in a country where they were slaves:

"O Nebuchadnezzar, we do not need to defend ourselves before you in this matter"[13].

It must have been from a heart-felt conviction based on their personal experience of the goodness of God and the greatness of His love and power.

Nehemiah had an enormous task before him because at that time he had no organization or system to support him in realizing the dream. In fact, he did not live in Jerusalem. The enemies of his people were around and about. Many of the enemies knew that the rebuilding of the wall would provide security for Jerusalem's inhabitants and be a defense for them. Their enemies did all they could to stop the project. Whenever the people of God in the Bible were obedient to God and united, they became a formidable force that no army could conquer. Their enemies knew this too. Nehemiah had not been a king before. He had no military training for all we know, and nothing suggests that he had any previous building skills. Ask anybody who knows and he would tell you that it takes more than being a cup-bearer of the king to rebuild the walls of a room!

John Maxwell says,

"If we cannot act alone, we cannot act together".

So the team begins with one person. That one person is the leader who has first overcome his personal fear of the problem ahead. He must be willing to continue if all that he has is himself and God. Deep conviction and faith in God is a prime preparation that a leader needs. There is a way to overcome every problem of life. You have to find it as the leader; you must be willing to give all that it will take to find it and work it through. Remember that you cannot give what you do not have and you will only be able to sell what you believe in. Challenges that naturally come along in life will reveal what you are made of.

Hardly does anybody find himself in a situation where all that will lead to accomplishing his dreams are in his backyard. Great achievers start with little or nothing till a door of opportunity is opened to them. Nevertheless, they walk on, persevering the course till they start to see their dream afar off. It does not matter how long or rough the road appears to be. Knowing that it leads to the dream is all that they need, to press on. The leader is the person who sees the end and knowing that the road he is on will lead to the end, goes on the road, refusing to be influenced by anything but the desire to achieve the envisaged end.

Lesson 4:
KEEP THE VISION

Vision is the end that is desired or expected; it is the driving force that keeps the team going. Vision is such a powerful ingredient that the word of God says without it, even God's people perish. Vision is more than carefully articulated words that describe what a people or organization does. Vision is from God. When vision is from men, it is ambition. A leader must be careful not to pass on ambition as vision. This is a common error that comes from walking in the flesh, or in man's understanding. Whenever the leader feels that he has the entire plan or knows how to get to the planned destination, the vision could become ambition.

The effectiveness of the vision in motivating people depends on how clearly it is communicated. This is a very basic principle that is missed over and over again. When an organization draws up its vision, it must break it down for each person in the organization so that every action that they take ties into the vision and moves the organization towards reaching the goal. When communication is unclear, actions intended to lead to the vision, may ultimately detract from the vision. No wonder then that Habakkuk was instructed to write down the vision and make it plain that "he might run, who reads it".

When vision is well articulated, it becomes like fire within anyone to whom it is addressed, such that after reading the vision, he gets a clear picture, which propels her/him onto the next level. Throughout scripture we see how God used this principle to move His people. To Abraham He said,

"I will make you into a great nation and I will bless you; I will make your name great and you will be a blessing"[14]. He added "I will surely bless you and make your descendants as numerous as the stars in the sky and as the sand on the seashore"[15].

To the children of Israel, He said of His mission and about their situation,

"I have come down to rescue them from the hand of the Egyptians and to bring them up out of that land into a good and spacious land, a land flowing with milk and honey"[16].

The way heaven is envisioned in scripture is that its streets are paved with gold and as a place where,

"He (God) will wipe every tear from their eyes. There will be no more death or mourning or crying or pain"[17].

God uses these pictures to motivate us and keep us focused on getting to the end.

A leader receives God's picture of the destination and some direction about how to get there. He then gets into moving towards it and shows the way to others. Being sold out to the vision makes the leader to dwell on the picture that he has received. He develops a better appreciation for it and can re-create it for anyone who wants to know about it. The Bible teaches that

"For as he thinketh in his heart, so is he"[18].

By going over the vision over and over again, the leader and the vision become inseparable and he is naturally stirring up passion for the goal in the followers.

A clear vision helps the leader see more and farther than any other person in the group. When the vision is not clear to the leader, he is easily distracted or persuaded to take decisions that are not in the interest of the group whether they be long term or short term. Very often, followers will come up with wonderful ideas of achieving some objectives. The leader by virtue of the perspective that he has is better able to judge how those actions may affect the future of the group.

Nehemiah had a picture of Jerusalem before the walls were destroyed and that was the starting point for him. He developed a clearer picture of the goal as he prayed to God. The vision was already put in place in God's word – Nehemiah 1 :9b

"If you return to me and obey my commands, then even if your exiled people are at the farthest horizon, I will gather them from there and bring them to the place I have chosen as a dwelling for my Name".

The vision was that God's people will return to Jerusalem; so the desolation was only temporary and the vision belonged to God who cannot fail.

Knowing the faithfulness of God, every vision that He gives is backed up with His resources and His word will not fall to the ground; it must accomplish its purpose. Get the vision and run with it! When the vision is blurred at the level of the leader, it can only be more blurred when it gets to the followers. Its impact is geometrically reduced, so that where a 100% clear vision leads to 100% goal attainment; a 90% clear vision will often lead to significantly less than 90% goal attainment. The clarity of the vision is related to how yielded the leader is. How was it that Elisha prophesied that:

"About this time tomorrow, a seah of flour will sell for a shekel and two seahs of barley for a shekel at the gate of Samaria"[19].

What he saw was very vividly impressed on him. Even though it seemed so far fetched in the light of prevailing circumstances, it was more than an impression on his spirit. He declared it with boldness.

Lesson 5:
THERE WILL BE SACRIFICES TO MAKE
Leadership demands sacrifice. Every leader will at one time or another sacrifice personal pleasure, comfort, aspirations and well being for the greater good of the people that he is leading. At any time, there are competing

demands for the resources at our disposal. Inability to satisfy all demands makes it imperative that priorities be set. As the top items on the priority list are being attended to, those lower in priority suffer. How should a leader order his resources? The most important of our resources is time. Time is the common resource at the disposal of all, but nobody can increase their portion of it or accumulate it. It is a wasting resource that requires careful use. You either use it effectively or it slips away.

It is quite ironic that time is what leadership requires the most and the leader has just as much as the led. Sacrificial leadership is borne out of love for the people and a deep passion to make a difference for the people. Rick Warren in his book The Purpose Driven Life, says that love is spelt T.I.M.E. For the Christian leader, our commitment to do what is pleasing to God, requires of us a high standard and model for others to emulate. Only love could have made Jesus come to earth and die for people who were living in disobedience to Him. It is possible to love because God commanded it. The combination of the God-kind of love and obedience to Him will make the leader be like Paul who urged us as believers to offer ourselves as living sacrifices wholly and acceptable unto God which is our reasonable service. Every Christian is indeed called to live for the Lord, according to the Lord's program for our lives.

Jesus taught a very important lesson in Matthew 6 when he said that no man can serve two masters. As a leader, there will be repeated demand for time and other resources. If the required time commitment is not made the expected goals will not be achieved. Giving attention to the people and their needs and generally maintaining a close contact with the people are critical aspects of leading. People recognize leaders whom they know understand them. Visionary leaders will set objectives that the followers may perceive or even consider unrealistic. In such situations, they will follow only where they believe that the leader has their interest at heart.

Selfishness sets the leader up for failure. Leadership by its nature connotes aggregation of resources and power and vesting of such resources and power in leaders. If the leader has not dealt with the natural selfish instincts, there is more than ample opportunity to please self and inevitably there will be failure. When the leader gives up what he has, God will ensure that he is promoted. Jesus gave up His heavenly home and position for sinners and God therefore exalted Him and gave Him

"The name that is above every name" – Philippians 2:9.

25

Nehemiah gave up his high paying job in the "White House" of his time. He went on to the unfamiliar business of building in a dangerous territory. His love and commitment to the people were obvious. God caused his master King Artaxerxes to give him materials for the work because of his faithfulness. He put all that he had into the project of building the wall to restore the dignity of his people.

At the end of the story, Nehemiah became the governor in Jerusalem. More than that, he had a godly heritage in scripture and today we learn from his life.

Lesson 6:
PREPARE FOR RISKS

Change always involves some risk taking. Ask a group of people what are the risks associated with working on a job that involves traveling and you will find a stream of reasons why nobody should consider taking such a job. The fear of the unknown keeps many people locked in and separated from their God intended purposes.

There must be millions of people who have not married because they fear that their marriages may not succeed. Many will not buy a home because they fear they will be unable to make the payments and many will not bring up great ideas because they fear what people will say. If you consider the risks, you will probably just remain in bed or may be in your mother's womb. As soon as we are born, we enter into a world full of risks. One good illustration of this is the recent Severe Acute Respiratory Syndrome (SARS) scare. In the areas that were affected, you are at risk as long as you breathe.

Some risks are definitely not worth taking, especially when there are safer ways of achieving the same objectives. A wise leader knows how to assess risks and prepares responses for the risks that confront the people. God is the one who can change all things and it is to Him that all risks should be addressed. Risks should not make the leader or any body for that matter afraid of failure because fear only makes failure certain. The philosopher, Seneca said

"It is not because things are difficult that we do not dare, it is because we do not dare that they are difficult."

Whatever has never been done is mystified and judged as being difficult or impossible. There could be risks and challenges to do them, but these do not make them impossible.

Precious things are neither obvious nor exposed. The most desired things in life have to be sought after and success is often wrapped in failure. Show me someone who has never failed and I will show you someone who has never tried. The willingness to take risks makes the difference between successful people and average people.

Esther is a Biblical example of risk taking. She needed to come before the king to save her people, even though the law of the land prescribed death for anyone who appeared before the king without being invited. She summed up her situation this way

"I will go to the king, even though it is against the law. And if I perish, I perish"[20].

Her situation was a matter of life and death. She could have continued to enjoy her position as queen while her people suffered or taken the risk which eventually made her a deliverer of her people. The risk became worth taking especially after she got the people to pray and fast on her behalf. If she had not been willing to take the risk of being sentenced to death according to the rule in the kingdom, her people would have remained in bondage and may have been destroyed with her. She gained honor and freedom for herself and the people, and by the grace of God she was not killed.

The anticipation of the satisfaction that would follow the accomplishment of the goal, to the glory of God, makes the risk worth taking. Success brings joy and everyone wants to belong in the camp of the successful. Risks may be real, but it should not be the focus of the believer, otherwise fear would set in and the joy of success would be lost. Jesus endured the cross because of the joy that was set before Him. He despised the shame of hanging on a cross – Hebrews 12:2. Risk taking based on knowledge and discernment is not recklessness.

Lesson 7:
WIN THE CONFIDENCE OF THE PEOPLE
Leaders need to be constantly reminded that all that is being done is for the people. Nothing done for the people can be valuable to them unless they want it. Sometimes they may not understand what is being done, but believe that the leader has insights they do not have and is working for their interest. People love to associate with other people who have common problems, circumstances or appear to be like them. David was running away for his dear life from Saul, but he found other "vagabonds" who wanted a new identity, flocking to him. It was out of these people that he built his army

and very close associates for his many battles. I dare say that it is unlikely that David ridiculed these men. Rather, he must have motivated and made them appreciate their good qualities and so forged a formidable army out of them.

Building a reserve of goodwill with the people we lead is so important for those times of human failings. David faced this situation when he got back to Ziklag with his soldiers and the Amalekites had raided the camp and taken away as captives, their wives and children. His men were enraged and considered stoning him. Their understanding of his character probably made them hold back till he made a decision on what to do next. To recover what they had lost was a daunting task, but David was determined not to let his people down. As the people trusted their leader and gave him their goodwill, he in return gave determination to their cause. The Lord had assured David that he would recover all that his enemies had plundered, but he had to be courageous and determined to pursue his enemies.

Goodwill is earned. Even where the people come under a leader for some desired benefits, they quickly forget their earlier situation once goodwill is lost. They expect the full commitment of the leader to their cause. Recognizing that the relationship is an equation that requires being kept in balance will help the leader stay in contact with the people and ensure that he provides appropriate responses to changes in the expectations of the people.

Determination ensures that we end up where we envisioned. Tough decisions and distractions are inevitable in a "fallen world". Some people will attempt to divert or derail the vision. Only those who are determined can stay the course. This does not mean that the vision may not accommodate changes, but changes should not be because of a lack of will to face risks or challenges. Determination of the leader is a motivation for the people.

Nehemiah had the vision of what could be done in Jerusalem for his people. He presented the vision to them and they received it gladly. Effective communication of the vision was pivotal in getting the people to accept it, but a committed man was needed to work it through. God stirred up the hearts of the people to buy into the vision and the people strengthened and supported one another in love to work the vision. They respected the leadership of Nehemiah. He enjoyed the goodwill of the people as they willingly followed his leadership in all areas, including their spiritual lives.

Lesson 8:
IT'S ABOUT SERVICE

Leadership is service to the people. Without the desire and attitude of service, a leader will struggle with the people whom he is called to lead. The attitude of service puts the leader on a new pedestal from which his perspectives on issues that arise are addressed in understanding without entangling the leader's emotions. The leader becomes a parent figure to the people. He can objectively analyze issues and maintain focus for the greater good of the people. To the good leader, love for the people is more important than love for position. Through service for the people, a leader wins the respect and good will of the people.

Service to the people was so graphically explained by our Lord Jesus in John 13, in the story of the "order of the towel". Summing up the teaching, He said,

"The greatest among you will be your servant."[21]

When Peter found it hard to understand why Jesus, their Master, would wash the feet of the disciples and was going to ask to be excused, Jesus told him he would have no part with Him. It is obvious that Jesus was determined to have only people who needed Him as His followers. He had to be of service to them, or He would not be their leader. Leaders must identify what service they would provide for the people. If there is a need and you are not equipped to meet that need, you are not the leader of the hour.

Leaders provide for their people what they cannot provide for themselves. To thrust oneself over a people is to ask for rebellion. Deep down, people resent being dominated. So if you organize people on your street into a group so you can have an office and there is no need common to the people, which can be solved through the group, it will not be long before the group will disperse. If individually, the people can meet their needs, the group will also disperse. What distinguishes leaders over their people is their resolve to serve the general good and put it ahead of the individual good. Without this, the leader is only filling in a gap. It will not be long before the true leader will emerge.

"Worship the Lord your God, and serve him only".

These are the words of Jesus recorded in Matthew 4:10. It is true that leaders have similar needs like the people. How then can they ignore their needs and focus on the corporate needs? The service of leaders must first be to

God. That re-arranges the equation to make available to the leader, a source for his personal needs - God, who is the source of all good things; He is the source of promotion, the very source of life. There can be no loss to the leader in this arrangement and the leader can serve with strength, joy and zeal.

Nehemiah sought to provide a dearly needed service of restoring the physical protection of his people. He first gave up his position; he was not self-seeking. What he desired was the rebuilding of the ruins of the city of Jerusalem to restore the physical defense of the people.

Lesson 9:
YOUR INTEGRITY IS CRITICAL
No word sums up the responsibility of the leader like integrity. The implications of being persons of integrity are deep and it is critical that all the implications of integrity are brought to bear on carrying out leadership responsibilities. A tree for the definition of integrity is provided below. I have left out any repeated meanings of the word. Each leader needs to study and imbibe the quality that each connotes, and if necessary seek the opinion of respected leaders on the import of these words and how to bring them to bear on leadership responsibilities.

Integrity is
Honesty – frankness, candor, openness
True – fact, certainty
Truthfulness – straight-fowardness, faithfulness, directness,
Accuracy
Honor – respect, admiration, credit, reputation, tribute
Veracity – reality, actuality, authenticity, genuineness, sincerity, trueness
Reliability – dependability, steadfastness, trustworthiness
Uprightness – decency, respectability, morality, honorableness, worthiness.

Integrity brings security to the leader and the people; see Proverbs 10:9. Think of how many leaders you know that have fallen because of some actions that were not done in integrity. Integrity of the leader assures the people of the leader's commitment to them and so they can place their trust in him. The leader is also secure, and so would not worry about strange accusations. He or She can go home each day with peace in his/her heart.

Closely related to integrity is transparency. Leadership puts people in the limelight, but many people are uncomfortable with transparency. Living a transparent life is not easy. Your every action will be scrutinized and evaluated. Being a transparent leader does not mean giving up one's privacy, rather it means not attempting to be unaccountable in any aspect of the responsibilities of leadership. When a leader chooses a transparent lifestyle, it provides security for the leader since his actions relating to the responsibilities of leading are openly done with no hidden agenda. You can openly justify any position that you take.

Integrity will take a leader farther than any other quality. Whatever is not done with integrity will pull down the reputation of the leader and can destroy him. A glass of clean water will promote health and wellbeing, but it becomes a killer once a drop of poison gets in it. Integrity maintains wholesomeness, completeness and authenticity; without it the leader becomes manipulative and self-seeking. A progression to every negative influence is inevitable when integrity is lacking.

Nehemiah kept account of his actions - that is how we got the book. He maintained a record of the resources – people, finances and materials used in the work. He could have easily ignored the records of what he received and how they were used. It was unlikely that King Artaxerxes would have been interested in the details because he was given a blank check to obtain materials for the work. A leader will do well to maintain a standard higher than what the people expect. Integrity is the leader's safeguard for keeping his reputation, future and testimony intact.

Lesson 10:
GOD IS YOUR PROVIDER

Provision makes pursuing the vision a pleasure. A leader has more than enough to be concerned about and so the assurance of provision makes the burden lighter. Provision connotes all that is needed to execute the vision. It is therefore logical (not only spiritual) that provision has God as the true source. No man can guarantee that all that would be needed to achieve a goal will be available, but God can. God can guarantee the future because He knows and owns all things. Wow, what a blessed assurance that God will come through and meet the needs of the vision, including those that the leader cannot envisage at present.

Wisdom and favor come from the Lord. Wisdom is the principal thing - as Solomon taught in the book of Proverbs 4:7. We know that our God is a God of wisdom, He says in His Word:

"If any of you lacks wisdom, he should ask God, who gives generously to all without finding fault, and it will be given to him"[22].

True wisdom comes from God and it is through prayer and obedience that a leader will receive this much-needed blessing. Favor distinguishes any person upon whom God has bestowed it. There may be ways that have been impossible for others to walk, but God in His favor can open the door for His favored one. The favor of God will put at the disposal of the leader, the power, resources and ability of God.

It is God who brings in resources through the people that He has brought and prepared to fulfill the vision. God's vision cannot be hindered by lack of any kind. God used an unbelieving King, Cyrus to provide for his work in Isaiah 45:1. It is clear that God chose the king, for He had previously given him control over resources, before He stirred his heart to provide the resources for His work. People do not need to be manipulated; their hearts are in the hands of God and only He can turn them towards what is pleasing unto Him.

Nehemiah's situation with King Artaxerxes is similar to the case of King Cyrus. Why would a king commit his resources to his cupbearer just because this usually jovial servant was sad for one day? One would have thought that the King would arrange some time off or a one-hour show by the court jesters to help Nehemiah brighten up or may be offer him a promotion or generous personal gift. God's intervention, made all the difference and the King rather sent him to go and re-build the walls of Jerusalem; gave him access to his forests for materials of construction, and security for the journey. Nehemiah recognized the hand of God at work – in Nehemiah 2:8, he said –

"And because the gracious hand of my God was upon me, the king granted my requests".

People need vision for their lives and if vision is of God, then God holds Himself responsible to provide for the vision. This may sound simple, but it is so true. The responsibility of seeking and working in the will of God remains that of the leader. Remember that God wants to maintain fellowship with His people. The role of leadership is to keep the people connected with the owner of the vision who is the provider for fulfilling the vision.

VI. DEALING WITH ADVERSARIES

There is hardly a program of significance or value that will not be challenged by people. Even where the purpose is clearly to the advantage of all, people will find reasons to disagree with the program. It could be that the time is not right for them or that they would rather do the same things by themselves or in another way, or that they had not been taken into confidence ahead of the program. When a leader appreciates this point, the fact that there are adversaries or opposition will not have a major influence on his resolve to move to the next level. What the leader wants to focus on is ensuring that adversaries do not take more than "the debt of love owed to all men", from the purpose at hand. Contending with the adversary must not be substituted for the principal goal of the group, neither should it become a principal activity of the group. It is a distraction that only needs to be dealt with as such. So what do you do when adversaries loom large over the vision so much so that it threatens the principal task of moving on?

When such is the case, it is time to get back to the owner of the vision for directions. In general, adversaries if handled with the right attitude will not be more than a distraction that eventually gets silenced. Let's look at Nehemiah's experience.

Sanballat and Tobiah were the main adversaries of Nehemiah,

"They were very much disturbed that someone had come to promote the welfare of the Israelites"[1].

Their first approach was to mock the people and what they were about to do. In Nehemiah 2: 19, it was recorded that they despised the people with Nehemiah and laughed them to scorn. This strategy did not succeed, for Nehemiah and his people had a strong resolve and did not allow the words of their enemies to affect them. At this stage, Sanballat and Tobiah and their company did not physically prevent the work. This was Nehemiah's answer to them:

"We His servants will start rebuilding, but as for you, you have no share in Jerusalem or any claim or historic right to it"[2].

He and the people ignored them and so did not allow the biting words of the adversary to affect their work and commitment. More discouraging, harsh words of the opposition are recorded in the book of Nehemiah

4:2 - "What are those feeble Jews doing? Will they restore their wall? Will they offer sacrifices? Will they finish in a day? Can they bring the stones back to life from those heaps of rubble, burned as they are?"

4:3 - "What they are building-if even a fox climbed up on it, he would break down their wall of stones!"

Seeing that mockery and unkind words were not working, the adversary resorted to a strategy of distracting Nehemiah by trying to pre-occupy him with frivolities. They invited Nehemiah to meet with them. Sanballat and Tobiah arrogated to themselves the authority they did not have. They were not elected or appointed officers, but they invited Nehemiah apparently to answer their queries. They were authority usurpers who had before now manipulated the people in their ignorance. Of course, Nehemiah knew what they intended to do; harm him either directly (physically) or indirectly (spiritually/ psychologically). His response was simple. He told them that he was doing a great work, and so he could not afford the luxury of meeting with them. They could have gone to him, but they wanted him in their territory because of their evil intentions.

Nehemiah's response was polite and in tune with their position. They could not make him honor their invitation and he was bold enough to turn it down regardless of the number of times they sent for him.

The one at work in the adversaries is of course the devil himself. We know, he does not give up easily. Sanballat and Tobiah moved on to a new level of intimidation and accusation. They now made up lies against Nehemiah, that he was organizing the people to rebel against the king and that Nehemiah planned to be king – see Nehemiah 6:7. The Scripture tells us that their intention was to break the resolve of God's people and stop the work. Nehemiah responded with prayer. He asked God to strengthen him and the people with him in the work. Again this enemy strategy did not succeed.

Physical attack on the people was then planned. Nehemiah 4:11 says -

"Before they know it or see us, we will be right there among them and will kill them and put an end to the work"

The adversaries became desperate. They were willing to kill in order that the work would stop. The enemy intended that Nehemiah and his people would not have a clue about this line of action. It was intended to surprise them. The Lord revealed the intention of Sanballat, Tobiah and their company to Nehemiah and he planned his response accordingly.

Nehemiah got the people together and communicated the situation to them. He used the opportunity to re-emphasize the importance of the work they were doing and encouraged them to continue diligently. He said in Nehemiah 4: 14

"Don't be afraid of them. Remember the Lord, who is great and awesome, and fight for your brothers, your sons and your daughters, your wives and your homes"

This scripture re-emphasizes the need not to give up in the face of adversity. The spirit that God has given His people is the spirit of courage, confidence in Him and power. The people had to be re-organized to ensure continuity of the work. Half of the people had to be deployed to watching and enhancing security while the other half continued the work.

Nehemiah was a man of wisdom and balance. He understood the principles of walking with God and his responsibilities as a leader. In 4: 20, He says

"Our God will fight for us".

This was the ultimate source of power and protection. And as a man of faith, he fully appreciated the need for being responsible to the people. He assigned half of his people to keep watch. The rest of the people were then armed in readiness for any eventuality from the enemy. Being timid would have been counter-productive and he demonstrated his resolve to confront the enemy if required. It was a tough and desperate situation and if they wanted to succeed, they would have to be tough and resolute and not back-down to the enemy. Throwing-in the towel was what the adversary wanted and he was determined not to do that.

Despite these hard conditions, Nehemiah arranged that the people started work early and did not stop till it was late. This was wisdom, because the longer the work took, the greater the opportunity the enemy had to stop it. He got his people to make the necessary sacrifice of personal comfort to achieve the goal of rebuilding the wall. They did not take off their clothes or relax and become complacent; they had their weapons on them always, no matter what they were doing.

Though he knew that God was with him and that victory over his adversaries was certain, Nehemiah did not take the enemy for granted. He made sure that the people were ready for any attacks. He sent a clear signal to the enemy that he intended to defend the work.

Through this we can see how God uses the adversities of life to make us better people. What the enemy wanted to use against Nehemiah got him to pray more; it made him to spend time going over the importance of the work with his people. This experience must have bonded the people more into a team with a clear understanding of their objective and a willingness to go all the way. There was no record of anyone withdrawing from the work. The adversaries must have become cautious too, as they did not attack Nehemiah and his people till the wall was completed.

By coming against God's people, the adversary made them to pray for strength, which they received from the Lord. The wall was completed in 52 days! This was record project completion period for a group of unskilled people who had only their efforts to give. God, working through the leader and the people gave wisdom, and despite the cutting back on the number of people building to provide security, the work was completed ahead of schedule. What the adversary meant for evil, God turned around for their benefit.

God's perspective of adversity makes all the difference in our lives. Prayer is a vital part of Christian living and sometimes, it would seem that peace and quiet in every area of our lives, dulls our prayer life. The promise of God concerning adversity is just beautiful and re-assuring.

"No temptation has seized you except what is common to man. And God is faithful; He will not let you be tempted beyond what you can bear. But when you are tempted, He will also provide a way out so that you can stand up under it"[3].

The appreciation of this promise will make us stand up against adversity. It helps us know that we are expected to go past it and not run from it. God knows how we should respond. We go to God in prayer therefore, obtain the response and act with confidence in the unfailing God. Thus equipped, we are able to cope and even overcome adversity. Praise the Lord!

While God commits to seeing us through adversity, we must commit to maintaining our resolve to walk with Him till we get to His ordained end. The enemies of Nehemiah had progressively dangerous strategies to stop him. It was important that his resolve was stronger than theirs. God remains unchanged, His purpose He will fulfill, but we can abort the plan of God for us by being faint-hearted. We can sum up Nehemiah's response to adversity in two parts – he made sure he did his part

God had put in his heart to rebuild the walls of Jerusalem – he was going to do it!

He was convinced that God would fight for them and they would be victorious over their enemies; and God will also do His part!

The two components of his response guided his every action. Amazingly adversity pushed him into quick completion of the task. This was an unexpected additional reward for his resolve. God wants to confound the enemy in their ways. He wants to display His manifold wisdom through obedient children who will stand, regardless of the arrows of the enemies.

"The creation waits in eager expectation for the sons of God to be revealed"[4]. *"We know that the whole creation has been groaning as in the pains of childbirth right up to the present time"*[5].

Human strength and wisdom is limited and ultimately fails. Through prayer, we access the unlimited and unfailing power of God. God's attributes of being all knowing, loving and caring to His obedient children become our heritage when we are walking by His leading.

Even after the wall was completed and dedicated, Sanballat and Tobiah did not give up. They continued to look for ways to discredit Nehemiah, his people and the work. Clearly, the devil was at work through them because nothing was sacred to them. They found Eliashib a relation of Tobiah who was the high priest, and got him to allow them the use of part of the storage room in the temple for the private business of Tobiah. They maintained close contact and were intent on gathering information to assist in working out a strategy for the downfall of Nehemiah.

Hitherto, the enemy and their company were all outsiders and their strategies and actions could easily be identified for their intents. The next and last strategy of the enemy was to infiltrate the ranks of Nehemiah's people. This is a very potent weapon that adversaries can use against a leader. The people with whom a leader has become comfortable with and trusts in, are prime targets for the adversary. The scheme is to make them believe that he (the adversary) is a better friend to them than the leader. How does this happen in a coherent group working with strong resolve? It is often through,

a)   changing the corporate goals to things that the people do not appreciate or accept - a disconnect between the leader and the led

b) the leader becoming unreachable to the people

c) rapid growth which results in a large number of the people (some of whom may become leaders too) with weak perceptions of the vision and purpose.

d) complacency of leaders, not maintaining and improving on the fellowship relationships shared

Mutating from a 'compatriot' to 'adversary within' is a slow process and the subject often may not realize at what point the change from friend to foe took place. Not being in agreement with others on issues, without seeking resolution of the same, is a seed that can grow into a schism. At other times, it is divided loyalty or an independent spirit that is not completely subjected to the leadership, which will begin the process of making one an adversary to what he had previously believed in. In the case of Eliashib, it was divided loyalty out of brotherly love or other similar reasons that made him yield to Tobiah.

Nehemiah was quick and decisive in dealing with the matter when it came to his attention. He removed Eliashib from his office and appointed another in his place. Some may say, "but nothing had happened and a warning could have been adequate." Most leaders however will view this sanction as appropriate.

Nehemiah was magnanimous and unprejudiced to allow Eliashib, a relation of Tobiah, a known adversary of the people, to become the priest in charge of the affairs of the temple. The betrayal of trust, in the light of the experiences of Nehemiah and the people with Tobiah, demanded that the matter be dealt with decisively, so that others may be deterred from similar actions. Eliashib's actions amounted to a coup-d'etat in the political arena.

So, What Does the Adversary Want?

Answering this question is very useful in dealing with adversaries. The hearts of men are open before God. Indeed, God does not judge with testimonies or words, He judges the intents of men's hearts. Asking God for revelation of the purposes of adversaries is the main way to receive the understanding of the problem. When the adversary planned to kill Nehemiah and his people, God revealed it.

But we also know from the Bible, that from the abundance of the heart, the mouth speaks. Leaders should pay very close attention to what their adversaries say or do. They will eventually reveal the motives behind the things that they do. Sanballat and Tobiah were exceedingly grieved that Nehemiah had come to seek the welfare of the children of Israel. Meaning that they benefited from the desolation of Jerusalem and the reproach of the people. They wanted to maintain the status quo.

Sanballat and Tobiah had nothing good to offer the people, while Nehemiah came to actualize God's vision for the people. This fact assured Nehemiah's victory over them.

The devil is behind confrontations from the adversary and it is the Lord Himself that will deal with your adversaries.

"When a man's ways are pleasing to the LORD, He makes even his enemies live at peace with him"[6].

VII. A WORD FOR FOLLOWERS

Leadership and followership go hand in hand; they are directly related and success of one leads to success of the other. Leaders are successful when their followers prosper or attain the goals that they have set. Without the followers, there would be no leaders and the leader provides the followers with what they are unable to provide for themselves. The relationship between the leaders and the followers is one of mutual dependence, respect and cooperation; the goal is one and it is attainable only when both are tugging in the same direction.

The connection between leaders and followers is a key determinant of the quality of relationship and the effectiveness of the group in their endeavor. Small groups enjoy the benefit of steady interaction between the leader(s) and the led. As the size of the group increases, it is common that matters affecting the well being of the whole group do not get aired. Tensions could build and may be aggravated by a long waiting period for the opportunity to air them. Where there are no deliberate arrangements for venting individual opinions, people may become disenchanted. What is most important is not that the ideas or opinions of everyone are followed, but that there has to be a flow of communication upwards and downwards. Horizontal communication amongst the leaders and the led is taken for granted, but in some situations it needs to be nurtured. There should be no situation where one hand does not know what the other is doing – if such a situation is allowed, the potential for conflict is increased.

Believe in your leader or you will not derive any benefits from his leadership.

"Listen to me, Judah and people of Jerusalem! Have faith in the LORD your God and you will be upheld; have faith in His prophets and you will be successful"[1].

Naturally each one of us wants to be in control of our circumstances and while being led requires relinquishing to someone else our right to make individual decisions, we should be relaxed about it and enjoy the transferred as well as shared responsibilities of belonging to the group. A group offers greater strength and capacity than any individual and that is what we intend to access by joining the group. An unwilling member of a group is a weak link that could frustrate the efforts of the group and so limit the potentials of the group.

When you belong, you should allow yourself to be led. Recognize that you have accepted to be guided by the way the group operates. For the believer, we are instructed in Hebrews 13:17 that we should ensure that our leaders are in a position to give account about us joyfully. This requires that we trust them and release ourselves to be guided while supporting them as much as possible. Remember that the leader is a person of limited capacity just like any other person. They attain success through other people whom they organize and direct to achieving set goals. However profound the abilities of a leader may be, he needs willing people to make a difference.

Give your leader your best at all times. The people that Nehemiah led were so exemplary in this. Nehemiah had reasons to push them to greater productivity. They were not skilled builders or warriors, but they were committed and cooperative people. Their attitude enhanced the work and freed their leader to tackle the hard issues of organizing the work and keeping their enemies at bay. They did not get involved in grumbling. When they had issues they brought it to the knowledge of the leader (for instance, when interest was charged by the more advantaged Jews to the point of creating a great burden for the poorer majority). Without doubt, they helped one another where possible and shielded the leader from mundane issues. They took care of the little issues in love.

There will be times of disagreement with the leader. The fact of life is that we are all different and our opinions are formed by our experiences and circumstances. Expect that you will sometimes disagree with your leader. At such times, seek an opportunity to make your position clearer. Where your opinion is not accepted or considered, you have further responsibility about the matter. You need to take it to the Lord in prayer.

God is the One who has put all leaders in authority. Not surprisingly, they are all firmly under His control.

"The king's heart is in the hand of the LORD; He directs it like a watercourse wherever He pleases"[2].

Water is easily manipulated and that is what the heart of the most difficult leader is in the hands of God. Many people may not agree with speed limits on the roads, but if there is to be a change, there is an established due process of changing that law. The law does not change on the highway, it is changed by an act of the legislature.

So also when we disagree with our leaders, we should show understanding by taking the matter to the Person who is able to change them and who made them leaders in the first place. You can confront the highest leader of whatever organization, by whatever name called in the presence of God. But remember that God is a just God, so what you have to bring must be just.

You owe your leader the debt of prayer. Leadership is a deep spiritual matter that can eternally affect the destinies of the followers. When we accept to come under the authority of a leader, we accept to be led and to follow the guidance provided. The leader is a person and every person changes. It is only God who is the same yesterday, today and forever. If people change, then a leader may start right, but soon get diverted or even derailed. It takes time for evidence of derailment to show. Remember Samson? There was no sign that the Spirit of God had left him till he tried to destroy his enemies as he had done in the past and found out that he could not – Judges 16:20. You need to pray that your leaders will remain on track, in God's presence, being obedient to Him and leading the people according to God's instruction to them.

Praying for your leader is praying for yourself. As long as we belong to a group, the leadership of the group is our location for God's blessing. It is in that place that God will prosper and establish us. We are corporately united and can be promoted or hindered by what goes on in the group. Praying for godly leaders will ensure that the atmosphere is right for the power of God to bring to pass our expectations. With the right leadership, even where people make mistakes, they will be corrected and the whole group will not suffer. Our leaders are mentors that God uses to help us identify our calling as well as provide encouragement when necessary, so that we will attain God's destiny for our lives.

There are leaders who are insecure. They find it hard to encourage their followers or help grow the gifts of God in them. We all have one Master – the Lord Jesus. When the leader learns from His example, he is able to develop a gift greater than what he has from within the group. Peter and John were able to acknowledge Paul, give him a hand of fellowship and encourage his gift to the gentiles. When the leader is generous at heart towards his people, they can pray as in Psalm 133 that the anointing of God will flow from his head to them all. Everyone is secure and unity thrives.

VIII. NUGGETS ON LEADERSHIP

Nugget 1:
BELIEVE IT, YOU ARE A LEADER!

Leadership is the ability or responsibility to influence the actions of others. In more ways than we realize, we are all leaders. Being conscious of our leadership roles will help us to be positive influences to the people that we lead. Our first leadership responsibility is also the most important – the family. Our family relations take our words and actions more seriously than any other person would. It is so important that we model the right attitudes and character to our families who are with us the most and thus are influenced most by our lifestyles.

Parents particularly, need to recognize and see themselves as leaders in the family. The import of having children is the acceptance of responsibility to lead them in the way of the Lord. Children learn principally from examples around them. Influences are so important to children, the impressions that are made on them define them and their character. Parents have the greatest opportunity to shape their children's lives as a result of the closeness and continuous interaction that they can have with them. The interaction that parents have with their children ultimately makes the children become like the parents. Where there is no interaction with parents, the void will be filled by outside influences and the children will also become like those they relate with.

In the Church, new members will take on the attitudes and style of the older members. The love of God and His people, commitment, and giving to the work of God of new members will be influenced most by the attitudes the older members exhibit. Being conscious of the far-reaching implications of our actions will help us to model the right attitudes. Paul is a good example to use in weighing the impact of our actions; he said that he would not eat meat if it would cause his brother to sin.

As members of the family of God, we have the responsibility to model lives that meet God's standards. Jesus said to us

"You are the salt of the earth"[1]. *"You are the light of the world"*[2].

He also said

"Let your light shine before men, that they may see your good deeds and praise your Father in heaven"[3].

This leadership responsibility is for all who have accepted Jesus as Lord and Savior. The most resounding message in every personal evangelism effort is a life that displays the new life that believing on the Lord Jesus gives.

Nugget 2:
LEARN THE VISION OF YOUR TEAM/GROUP

To be productive or valuable to a group, the first and most important requirement is to learn the vision. It would appear to be an obvious requirement, but particularly in the Church environment, we find many members who have no understanding of the vision of the assembly to which they belong. It is quite true that our purpose in Church is to serve the Lord. Our service however needs to be defined if it is to be real. Every assembly has a focus of what it emphasizes in the service of God. As a member, find out what the focus of your assembly is. In other words, what the group is seeking to do within the larger body of believers and in society at large.

The vision belongs to God and we must remember that the leader is also human. The Word of God is the unchanging standard and all vision must clearly be derived and maintained on the Word of God. This calls for vigilance and diligence on the part of both leaders and followers. When deviations come up they should be discussed openly and every opportunity to resolve them in love explored.

Lack of knowledge or a poor understanding of the vision of the group to which one belongs easily leads to conflict. There are of course various activities that are general to all groups of believers, for instance, walking in love with all men. However a ministry could focus on teaching the word and building up its people, while another could focus on helping the needy. The vision is a prime influence on how the ministry allocates resources and therefore what is given priority.

Every group does not begin with all the people that are needed to realize the vision. So when the pioneers receive and share the vision, the fact that they cannot realize it all by themselves should make them write down the vision as we are instructed in Habakkuk 2. Writing the vision down makes it possible for joiners to read and run with it. When the vision is not written or documented, it gives room for the vision not to be definite or for other appendages that are not part of the vision to be added. When joiners learn the vision, it makes them of one mind with the pioneers and brings the power of unity to bear on the work of the group.

For instance a group could be started to pray for a nation and joiners may soon start requesting that time be made to pray for individual needs. The leader must be courageous enough to make it clear why such needs will need to be addressed elsewhere if the group is to stay focused.

Nugget 3:
IDENTIFY WITH THE PEOPLE

Leadership is about helping people to recognize their place in God. It helps people identify their true needs and shows them who can meet them. Many believe that no person can know the needs of another more intimately than the person who has the need. Even in situations where the needs of a people may be obvious to the leader, the people need to recognize it as such, otherwise, the leader may be seeking to fill a need that the people do not want met.

To know the needs of a people, leaders must identify with the people. Often, the leader is at an advantage in some way. Either they have received knowledge or wisdom from God, or have resources or exposure that the rest of the people do not have. The successful leader needs to continuously associate with the people, seek not to be separated or removed from them and see himself or herself as not being different from the others. Nehemiah was privileged to work for King Artaxerxes who was in a position to help in the reconstruction of the wall. Though he became governor in Jerusalem, he focused on being a Jew and fulfilling the purpose of God for his people and their generation. He was driven by a passion to restore the people to God so they could enjoy the benefits of being God's chosen people.

No matter how selfless a leader is, if the people do not perceive that he is one of them, they will be unable to work with him with singleness of heart. Identifing with the people that you lead wins their commitment and motivates them. A leader who wants to look good regardless of the situation of his people will find that the people are following very far behind or not at all. The ability to influence may be available, but the impact will be weaker than it can be.

Nugget 4:
DELEGATE RESPONSIBILITY AS NECESSARY

A good leader is able to reproduce himself in the people that he leads. Since leadership qualities are skills that are learnt and developed, good leaders will give sufficient attention to building up subordinates to fill in for them whenever it becomes necessary. The survival of the group is hinged on a good succession plan. After all, the leader is human too.

Leaders who are afraid to delegate curtail their overall capacity since they must personally oversee every activity or department. Delegation frees the leader to focus on the major issues; this keeps the group on track better than would have been possible if they were involved in detail management activities. Delegating tasks to others provides a means for the leader to better assess the qualities of people that they lead and in the Church setting, it helps the spiritual growth and maturity of the people. Inadequate delegation restricts overall capacity, it stunts growth and prolongs goal attainment.

Delegation of authority is a principle that God uses. All authority belongs to God, but He allows righteous and unrighteous men and women to use it. When God delegates, He allows the full exercise of the authority by those to whom they have been delegated. God defines the scope and holds those to whom He has delegated His authority accountable. True delegation provides a conducive and free environment for the subordinates to operate within reasonable boundaries. Delegation provides other people with opportunity to bring new influences and approaches to reaching the objectives. It brings variety and refreshes the system.

Nugget 5:
BE REAL
People want to follow someone who is like them. It is easier to follow someone whom you know understands your situation from having gone through it. If someone wanted to teach you how to survive in the African jungle, you would immediately want to find out if they have been out there in the jungle. Nobody can tell the story of war like a soldier who has fought in one. No matter how much you know about war and the techniques of war, the reality of being a target for the enemy is chilling – it can only be known from experience.

This was why Jesus Christ came into this world as a child. He had parents and grew up like every human and learnt to live life like any other person of His time. Though He could have come in glory and power He came as one of us so that we can recognize Him as one of us. He identified with us first so that we may identify with Him. He is our High Priest who knows our weaknesses as deeply as we know them (see Hebrews 4) because He has been there. He left this example for every leader. The closer you are to the people the more impact you can make in their lives and the more easily the goal will be reached.

Being real means being authentic. The leader is also a human being. The leader is fallible and should not become defensive when he makes mistakes.

He should rather be open about it. A leader who makes a mistake and admits it will endear the people to himself/herself more than a leader who seeks to cover up his/her mistakes. A leader must remember that leadership is often for a limited period. You will always need your friends and relationships so maintain the ties and even improve on them while leading them or other people.

When a leader is not being real, it creates a division between the leader and the people. This leads to a situation where the people see themselves as being on one side and the leader on the other. This feeling changes perspectives and opinions and soon unity is gone and the end is easily predictable –

"Every kingdom divided against itself will be ruined, and every city or household divided against itself will not stand"[4].

Nugget 6:
MAINTAIN A BALANCE IN YOUR LIFE

Though you are a leader, you are also being led; your leader is the Holy Spirit. Always remember that as you expect your followers to carry out their responsibilities so are you also expected to be responsible to your leader. Your leadership is limited in scope and responsibilities. You are at one place at any time and cannot be fully accountable for the people that you lead. For the leader, the one who leads you is fully accountable for you, for He knows your every move, and watch it - your every thought!

Maintain a balanced work ethic. Being a leader calls for above average dedication to the goal. Within the group, no one will hold a leader to specified daily work hours. Flexibility of work schedule is needed for effectiveness, but the responsibility of leadership is to deliver more than is required. There will be 20-hour days and there will be opportunities for relaxation, but through it all the leader is alert and responsive to the people as duty may require. A good leader is not so consumed with the vision that he neglects to make time for family, recreation and learning. This refreshes the leader and the people they lead. In Nehemiah 8:10, Nehemiah said to the people

"Go and enjoy choice food and sweet drinks, and send some to those who have nothing prepared. This day is sacred to our Lord. Do not grieve, for the joy of the LORD is your strength".

This was after the work had been completed, He recognized that there needed to be a time to refresh, appreciate and celebrate God's favor on the work.

Nothing can substitute for the leader's personal relationship with God. This is also true for his relationship with his family. There can be no excuse good enough to allow for a poor relationship with God or family. Time is the resource needed for maintaining both relationships; time has to be made available for these critical responsibilities. It is dangerous not to make time for these two relationships, because the effect may not be obvious till it is too late. Often lack of time for prayer and studying the word is a result of poor delegating. The leader should aim to do only what they must do. Keep seeking out new talents among the people and utilizing the talents of your people. There will be people who can do many things better than you can, encourage them to do it.

Nugget 7:
BE DECISIVE

Tough decisions are the daily routine of leadership. Be prepared for hard decisions that sometimes need to be made quickly. The leader must be fair and decisive. When Jesus came into the temple in Matthew 21 and met the people buying and selling, He did not have to go through a long process of investigation. He was decisive. He chased them out immediately. Nehemiah too was confronted with a similar situation where Eliashib, the priest was desecrating the temple by allowing Tobiah his cousin to use portions of the temple for his private affairs, Nehemiah had to remove Eliashib and replace him.

When situations of flagrant abuse of power or office by subordinates or other actions that detract from the vision of the group occur, they must be dealt with decisively or they can destroy the group as a whole. The leader must not toy with sin. Love the people, but make it clear that sin will not be tolerated. A leader who is not decisive in dealing with sin will unwittingly promote sinful living among the people. Sin is very destructive to a group and the leader needs to show clear example of how to deal with sin - cut it off from its roots.

Achan in Joshua 7 caused a similar problem for the Israelites when they went against their enemy. Because of his sin, God's people were defeated by their enemies and thirty six lives were lost that day. Sin can be very costly. It is the responsibility of the leader to protect the people under his care. The life of the leader also reflects in the people. When a leader condones laziness, immorality and disobedience to the laws (of God and man), he or she will find that it will permeate the group and will without doubt destroy the group.

Strong character is not opposed to love, indeed a strong Godly character is love.

"Do not despise the LORD's discipline and do not resent His rebuke, because the LORD disciplines those He loves as a father the son he delights in"⁵.

The leader should not be afraid to punish wrong. It is the instrument from God for helping the people get back on track. God's word is given for this purpose too.

Nugget 8:
PROVE YOURSELF AS A LEADER IN THE FAMILY

Your leadership must first be proven in your home. You must succeed in leading your own home, to be a success at leading other people. No wonder the Bible requires of people who will be leaders in the Church that they must be people who have their homes under good control. Whether we like it or not, the quality of leadership that one provides either as the head of the family or even as an older sibling is of interest to the people who are to follow after you.

Young people are influenced most by their parents and older siblings. Naturally, God has placed us all in positions of leadership, and if we do not consciously use those positions to make positive contributions to the lives of others, we are indicating that we are not prepared for additional leadership responsibilities. Our faithfulness in the "little" leadership roles qualifies us for the "greater" leadership responsibilities. As believers, we must be conscious of the influence we are on the lives of the people around us.

Unbelievers will first read our lives and it will influence their decision on whether or not to accept Jesus Christ as their Lord and Savior. Our commitment will influence their commitment after they decide to follow the Lord. Leaders lead in the moment, making every thought, every action and spoken word count for the benefit of the people around. When a servant is found faithful, he is entrusted with more responsibilities.

The word of God clearly instructs in 1 Timothy 3:1 that it is alright to seek the office of the bishop. The teaching of that scripture can be summed up in a few words: that whoever seeks the office of the bishop must first be a shepherd of his home. The call to lead one's home is universal and till a person has mastered this first requirement there can be no promotion to the next level of leading other people.

IX. CONCLUSION

Although separated by more than two millennia, the similarities of the world of Nehemiah and ours are striking. In fact, we stand a much better chance to influence other people and the world than Nehemiah, given the technological advancements now at our disposal. God's clarion call for "accomplished workers" has never at any time ceased. Rather the call is, in our days, much louder, and clearer.

"Whom shall I send? And who will go for us?"[1].

Who is an accomplished worker? Certainly the one who commences his God given assignment beautifully well with great excitement, continues with resolute determination and completes the assignment excellently with joy. He is the one who can say like Paul

"I have fought the good fight, I have finished the race, I have kept the faith"[2].

Other people will surely attest to this assertion too.

"There are three kinds of Christian leaders" said someone with a very vivid imagination.

A. "Canal barges" who, like boats need to be dragged and begged to work. Though they support the work, on the whole, one willing volunteer is worth five reluctant and pressed workers. (Act 9:6)

B. "The sailing ships" make fine going as long as there are no winds or storms. When things get hard and difficult, and the wind blows, they quickly turn back. (Col. 4:14; 2 Tim. 4 :9)

C. "The Atlantic Liner" type of workers are men and women who fight their way through wind and tempest because within them burns the mighty furnace of the love of Christ. (Acts 20:24; 21: 12-13)

Nehemiah, whose name means "YAHWEH COMFORTS" is a model of an accomplished worker to all Christians and even non-Christian leaders of all generations. Nehemiah, who is the principal character in this book commenced, continued and completed his God-given assignment brilliantly and in record time.

"So the wall has finished in the twenty-fifth day of Elul, in fifty-two days. When all our enemies heard about this, all the surrounding nations were afraid and lost their self-confidence, because they realized that this work had been done with the help of our God"³.

Nehemiah as a model of an accomplished worker is remarkable not only because of his outstanding qualities (which speak volumes of inspiring messages to us), but also because of his background. Nehemiah was neither a priest nor a prophet. He was not even the son of a prophet. In fact like Belteshazzer, Hananiah, Mishael and Azariah (popularly known as Daniel, Shadrach, Meshach and Abednego) nothing was known about him in Judah before his captivity to Babylon in 605 B.C.

Nehemiah, like the four Hebrew children, secured a very good job in exile. He was the Chief Security Officer to King Artaxerxes of Persia in 464-424 B.C.

"I was the king's cupbearer"⁴.

Nehemiah was a believer in Yahweh. His modest life and uncompromising faith in Yahweh made him a beacon among hundreds of his feeble-minded Hebrew fellows and Persians. His faithfulness in duty and loyalty to his heathen Persian King coupled with the favor of God no doubt secured for him the most sensitive job in the palace of Artaxerxes. What a testimony!

Nehemiah adorned the gospel with untarnished conduct, uncontaminated testimony and an undefiled life. He honored God by his life of implicit obedience to God. God in return also honored him

"Far be it from me! Those who honor me I will honor, but those who despise me will be disdained"⁵.

We live in the days when many so-called Christians do not adorn the gospel on their lives and conduct. Some people believe because they are not Pastors or "leaders" in the church, they can live anyhow. Some do not consider it imperative for them to be faithful in their secular assignments. The mentality of just doing enough to get by, still lingers with them. These folks can learn from Daniel about whom it is written.

The administrators and the satraps tried to find grounds for charges against Daniel in his conduct of government affairs, but they were unable to do so. They could find no corruption in him, because he was trustworthy and neither corrupt nor negligent. Finally these men said,

"We will never find any basis for charges against this man Daniel unless it has something to do with the law of his God"⁶.

The following attributes and their implications and ramifications qualified Nehemiah as a remarkable and reputable accomplished worker and leader. They should be the life standard and qualities of every believer.

PASSION

Passion is described as an ineffable and powerful love for God and man. Passion is much more than sympathy. Passion for man will compel one not only to see their need but also to do all within one's ability to solve the problems. No wonder, Jesus was known as a man of great compassion.

"When He (Jesus) saw the crowds, He had compassion on them, because they were harassed and helpless, like sheep without a shepherd"⁷.

Nehemiah was a man of great passion for his battered and devastated brethren in Jerusalem. When he heard about their suffering:

"When I heard these things, I sat down and wept. For some days I mourned and fasted and prayed before the God of heaven"⁸.

Please take note that Nehemiah was not mourning, weeping, fasting and praying for himself. He was well placed in the palace of the king. He was mourning, fasting and praying for many days because of his suffering brethren in Jerusalem.

"So be on guard! Remember that for three years I never stopped warning each of you night and day with tears"⁹.

Paul Yonggi Cho of Seoul, South Korea was won for Jesus by a young missionary through her compassion. Yonggi Cho did not believe at the initial stage of his confrontation with the gospel; he turned the young missionary away. As the missionary was leaving, she looked at him with tears rolling down her face. Her passion attracted Yonggi Cho's attention and he responded.

"If I do not believe the story you are telling me, I will believe because of your tears."

Today, Yonggi Cho pastors the largest single congregation in the world with over 800,000 members.

PRAYER

"Prayer is talking to God about man." We often sing that beautiful chorus - "Prayer is the key." Yes, prayer is the key to success in God's work. A. P. Gibbs says "He who will talk to man about God, must first of all talk to God about man."

Nehemiah was a man of fervent prayer. Let me say this, "Your passion will be dictated by the fervency and frequency of your prayer life." If you have no passion for souls, your prayers for souls will be listless and infrequent.

Nehemiah prayed anywhere and at anytime.

"The king said to me, 'What is it you want?' Then I prayed to the God of heaven"[10].

A.P. Gibbs says: "A prayerless Christian is not only a powerless but also a profitless Christian." He therefore exhorts us "to add kneeology to our Theology".

PURPOSE

Nehemiah was a man of distinguished purpose. He had a life-goal that he pursued rigorously with all his ability. You need to have a vision for your life, else you will live a purposeless life. (Nehemiah 2:5-6; 12:17; 6:15)

Paul said in the midst of pressures from friends and brethren:

"However, I consider my life worth nothing to me, if only I may finish the race and complete the task the Lord Jesus has given me – the task of testifying to the gospel of God 's grace"[11].

PERSEVERANCE

Nehemiah was a man of great endurance as he sailed through oceans of:

a)   Mockery - Nehemiah 4: 1-6

No matter how spiritual one is, his enemies will not see any good in him. Yes, his adversaries will slander and mock him as they did to our master, Jesus Christ.

b)   Conspiracy – Nehemiah 4:7-23

Failure to succumb to the enemies' mockery will result in conspiracy. Conspiracy may mount high around you from your enemies, but it cannot thwart the purpose of God for your life.

c)   Extortion - Nehemiah 6:1-4.

As Nehemiah faced the enemies externally, also he was surrounded by greedy nobles who continued to oppress and suppress the less privileged ones among them. What a problem!

d)   Compromise - Nehemiah 6:1-4

Because Nehemiah would not yield to the threats of the enemies; he was finally offered a compromise. This is the strategy of Satan. Beware of offers for compromise from the devil. Just as Moses refused all the compromises from Pharaoh, so you and I need to reject any offer of compromise from the devil, our spiritual enemy.

e)   Slander - Nehemiah 6:5-9

This is another subtle weapon of the enemy. No matter how good, gracious and gifted a man of God is, his enemies will slander him. The Pharisees accused Jesus of healing and casting out demons by Beelzebub (Luke.11:15).

f)   Treachery - Nehemiah 6: 10-14

False prophets and prophetesses abound in our day. They see visions of death, dangers, etc for their victims. We must beware of such false prophets (Matthew 24:5).

g)   Tribulations - 2 Timothy 3: 10-12

The afflictions and tribulations of the righteous are many. Thank God the afflictions will be used by the Holy Spirit to draw us nearer to God than ever before.

"It was good for me to be afflicted so that I may learn your decrees"[12].

Paul was drawn closer to God through tribulations (2 Corinthians 11:22-33). The Bible says *"In fact everyone who wants to live a godly life in Christ Jesus will be persecuted"[13]*.

PEOPLE

Nehemiah was a man of the people. He loved the people – Nehemiah 2:18. He served them and his people too loved him. They saw true love in him and they responded with hearty co-operation. We need to love the people of God that we lead sincerely and dearly.

GOOD POLICY

Nehemiah made many good and God glorifying reforms.

- He dissociated himself from the greedy nobles - Nehemiah 5:6; Leviticus 19:10; 23:22

- He restored the priests' positions – Nehemiah 13:13-24

- He hallowed the Sabbath day - Nehemiah 13:13-24

- He discouraged unholy alliances and marriages with non-Jews. Nehemiah 13:22-28; 2 Corinthians 6:14-18.

PURITY

Purity is holiness unto the Lord - Hebrews 12: 14. Nehemiah was a man of purity who hated sin and all evil, and who did all the known will of God. Nehemiah 13:31; 11:44-45; Isaiah 52:11; Genesis 39:9; 2 Timothy 2:19-21; 1 Peter 1:15-16 and Hebrews 12:14.

- Holiness is our honor. 1 Thessalonians 4:4 - Holiness places great honor on us before man and God. Daniel 2:46; 5:2; Revelation 1:6
- Holiness makes us illustrious sons and daughters of God - Exodus 28:1; Philippians 2: 14
- Holiness distinguishes us from sinners - 2 Timothy 2:19
- Holiness gives boldness in God - Proverbs 28:1; Daniel 3:16-17; 6:10
- Holiness leads us to heaven - Hebrews 12:14

Now let us like Nehemiah, take our God-given assignment to the next level where God is waiting to meet us. May you be richly blessed.

BIBLE REFERENCES

All references are from the New International Version of the Bible; where a different version is used it is annotated as such.

WHY STEP UP?

1. Genesis 17:1b (King James Version)

2. Deuteronomy 2:3 (New Living Translation)

3. Lamentations 3:22-23

4. Proverbs 4:18

5. John 15:5

6. Proverbs 25:2

7. I Corinthians 2:9

8. Luke 12:32

9. Psalm 75:6

HOW NEHEMIAH DID IT?

1. Nehemiah 2:12

2. I Samuel 2:9b

3. Nehemiah 2:17-18

4. Genesis 11:6; Psalm 133

5. Nehemiah 2:18

6. Nehemiah 2:20

7. Nehemiah 3:5

8. Nehemiah 5:16

9. Nehemiah 4:13

10. Nehemiah 4:4

NEHEMIAH'S DISTINGUISHING CHARACTERS

1.Nehemiah 5:11

2.Nehemiah 13:28

3.Nehemiah 7:2

4.Nehemiah 10:29

5.Nehemiah 10:30

6.Nehemiah 10:31

7.Nehemiah 10:32

8.Nehemiah 10:31

9.Nehemiah 10:35

10.Nehemiah 10:36

11.Nehemiah 10:37

12.Nehemiah 1:4-11

13.Nehemiah 5:19; 6:14, 22b & 29

TEN LIFE LESSONS FROM NEHEMIAH

1.Acts 15:18 (King James Version)

2.Psalm 121:4

3.2 Chronicles 16:9

4.Hebrews 13:8

5.Romans 12:2

6.Zachariah 4:6

7.I Samuel 2:9

8.Proverbs 21:1

9.Romans 8:24

10.II Timothy 1:7

11.Proverbs 28:1

12.Numbers 13:33

13.Daniel 3:16

14.Genesis 12:2

15.Genesis 22:17

16.Exodus 3:8

17.Revelation 21:4

18.Proverbs 23:7 (King James Version)

19.II Kings 7:1

20.Esther 4:16

21.Matthew 23:11 & John 13:16-17

22.James 1:5

DEALING WITH ADVERSARIES

1.Nehemiah 2:10

2.Nehemiah 2:20

3.I Corinthians 10:13

4.Romans 8:19

5.Romans 8:22

6.Proverbs 16:7

A WORD FOR FOLLOWERS

1.II Chronicles 20:20

2.Proverbs 21:1

NUGGGETS ON LEADERSHIP

1.Matthew 5:13

2.Matthew 5:14

3.Matthew 5:16

4.Matthew 12:25 & Mark 3:25

5.Proverbs 3: 11-12

CONCLUSION

1.Isaiah 6:8

2.2 Timothy 4:7

3.Nehemiah 6:15-16

4.Nehemiah 1:11

5.I Samuel 2:30

6.Daniel 6:4-5

7.Matthew 9:36

8.Nehemiah 1:4

9.Acts 20:31

10.Nehemiah 2:4

11.Acts 20:24

12.Psalm 119:71

13.II Timothy 3:12.